TRY THIS!

WET & WILD EXPERIMENTS FOR THE MAD SCIENTIST IN YOU

KAREN ROMANO YOUNG

PHOTOGRAPHS BY MATTHEW RAKOLA

NATIONAL GEOGRAPHIC

WASHINGTON, D.C.

WET&WILD

It glows. It flows. It shows up in different forms in unexpected places. You can even use it to make friends—or enemies. (Be careful who you trick!)

HIGHLIGHTED WATER
PAGE 6

WATER BEADS
PAGE 11

LIGHT-UP ICE BALL
PAGE 4

RAIN CLOUDS IN A BOTTLE
PAGE 9

LIGHT-UP ICE BALL

So pretty I've still got both of ours in the freezer.

HOW LONG IT TAKES
two days

WHAT YOU NEED
medium-size balloon (We used round
ones, but you can try other things.)
LED
electrical tape
battery casing with wire leads attached
AA battery
bowl
rubber band
needlenose pliers
paring knife or fingernail clipper

Water balloons + glowing lights + electronics + ice = a science experiment so cool and so inspiring we should charge admission!

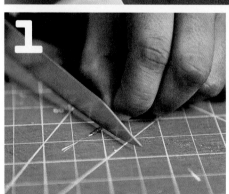

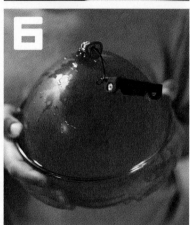

DAY ONE:

1 USE THE PARING KNIFE or fingernail clippers to remove ½ inch (1.3 cm) of insulation from the tips of the wire leads on the battery casing.

2 ATTACH THE POSITIVE (black) wire to the negative (shorter) end of the LED wire. Attach the negative (red) wire to the positive (longer) end of the LED wire.

3 TEST THE BATTERY. If it lights the LED, go ahead and wrap your connections in electrical tape.

4 INSERT THE LED in the balloon, leaving the battery casing outside.

5 FILL THE BALLOON with water, letting it expand like a water balloon. Use a rubber band to fasten the balloon's neck, leaving the battery and casing wired to the LED inside the balloon.

6 PLACE THE WATER balloon in a bowl and freeze it.

DAY TWO:

7 REMOVE THE ICE balloon from the freezer. Use a knife point to pierce the skin of the balloon, and peel the balloon off the ice.

WHAT TO EXPECT You should be able to see your LED's light shining through the ice that surrounds it. Isaac tested ours in a dark room.

WHAT'S GOING ON? Insulated wires, with connections protected with electrical tape, work fine with water surrounding them. The ice can obscure—or magnify and add sparkle to—the LED light.

- Which light is brighter—the LED by itself or the LED in ice?
- How would this project work with a balloon of a different shape?

HIGHLIGHTED WATER

Make your own Lake Eerie!

CONCEPTS

FLUORESCENCE, ULTRAVIOLET LIGHT

HOW LONG IT TAKES
one hour

WHAT YOU NEED
for blue:
tonic water, laundry detergent, or petroleum jelly

for other colors:
fluorescent-colored highlighter pens
water
knife
cutting board
rubber gloves
black or ultraviolet light or lightbulb

We can't quit coming up with variations on the theme of water that glows in the dark. How about the water beads (page 11) with glowing water? Would they absorb the colors of this fluorescent fluid? Or the ice ball (page 4), with glowing water—frozen, of course!—instead of plain? Here are some different ways to get that glow.

1 MAKE BLUE: Tonic water glows very brightly when exposed to black or ultraviolet light. The quinine in the tonic water makes it glow bright blue under black light. We found that petroleum jelly (such as Vaseline) makes a dull blue glow, but certain laundry detergents glow brightly.

2 MAKE OTHER COLORS: Fluorescent dye can be extracted from a nontoxic highlighter pen, but some experimentation (and pen sacrifice) is needed. You'll need a sharp knife and a cutting board. Cut a highlighter pen in half (the short way). Pull out the ink-soaked felt/plastic-coated fibrous tube. Remove the tube with the ink and slice it open so that the ink can flow out of the fibers. You can soak the ink pad in water for a few hours or use gloved hands to squeeze the ink that is inside the pen into water. Soak the felt in a small amount of water.

> WHAT TO EXPECT: The liquid you create will glow in the dark when exposed to black light or ultraviolet light. You may need to experiment with different types and colors of highlighters before you find the ones that work the best.
>
> Extra: Now you can add this dye to more water to make glowing fountains, grow certain kinds of glowing crystals, make glowing bubbles, or make glowing water beads.

> WHAT'S GOING ON? Fluorescent compounds—such as quinine and chemicals in highlighters—absorb highly energetic but invisible ultraviolet light and release less energetic visible light. The water is transparent so it is easy to color with these glowing chemicals.
>
> Note: You can store the glowing water in a sealed container and it will not go out or fade.

BONUS:
GLOWING HANDS

This isn't really an experiment, but it's so cool that it's irresistible. Use petroleum jelly (such as Vaseline) or laundry detergent on your hands. Put them up to a black light, and they should glow blue.

RAIN CLOUDS IN A BOTTLE

Done right, this one has the most rewarding whoosh.

CONCEPTS

WEATHER, CONDENSATION, PRESSURE

> HOW LONG IT TAKES
about twenty minutes

> WHAT YOU NEED
two-liter soda bottle, clean and dry (It's better with the labels removed, because you can see into the bottle clearly.)
rubbing alcohol
bicycle pump with needle
cork
skewer, drill bit, big needle, or something else you can use to make a path for the pump needle to go through the cork
optional: duct tape

For a better audience reaction to this action, work on your storytelling. How well can you explain the science behind the spectacle? (For hints, turn the page.)

RAIN CLOUDS IN A BOTTLE (CONTINUED)

WHAT TO DO

1-2

1 **FIT YOUR CORK** to your bottle. You may need to shave the sides off the cork to get a tight fit. Your aim here is the tightest possible seal.

2 **TRIM THE CORK** to the length of the bike pump needle. You want the needle to be able to pass through the cork into the bottle, maintaining a tight seal.

3 **MAKE A PATH** for the cork, using your skewer, drill bit, or needle. Be sure the object you use to pierce the cork is narrower than the bike pump needle, or you won't have that tight seal I keep talking about.

5

4 **WHEN THE CORK** is ready, take it out of the bottle.

5 **POUR ONE TEASPOON** (5 mL) of rubbing alcohol into the bottle and screw the cap back on.

6 **WITH THE CAP ON,** turn the bottle horizontal and roll it so that the alcohol sloshes around and coats the inside of the bottle thoroughly and evenly.

7 **INSERT** the cork.

8 **INSERT THE BIKE PUMP** needle in the cork.

9 **PUMP THE BIKE PUMP** four or five times. Sometimes when you do this the cork will blow and you'll have your reaction. Other times you'll have to pump a few times more, then stop and pull the needle out.

6

7

8-9

WHAT TO EXPECT Once the pressure is released—either because the cork blows or the needle is removed—a cloud should form quickly and dramatically in the bottle.

Note: Aim the bottle away from you and anyone else. When Aaliyah pumped hard, our cork shot out and nearly hit Marco.

GLITCH? No cloud? Your seal isn't tight enough. Try a different cork, or use duct tape around the mouth of your bottle to tighten the seal.

WHAT'S HAPPENING? You're mimicking the part of Earth's water cycle in which evaporated water (water vapor) cools and condenses, forming clouds as they connect with dust. In this experiment, the alcohol acts like the dust, providing something cool for water droplets to attach to.

When you pressurize the soda bottle by pumping air in, the air molecules collide with each other and warm the bottle. Releasing the pressure causes the water vapor to condense quickly, forming a cloud.

BONUS

REVERSE THE EXPERIMENT!

Before the cloud disappears, put the needle back in and pump a couple more times. The cloud should disappear as quickly as it came. Release the pressure, and the cloud will re-form.

NOTE ABOUT
WATER BEADS
They are sold under
lots of different
brand names,
including Water
Gems and Orbeez.

WATER BEADS

An absorbing experience

CONCEPTS

POLYMERS, ABSORPTION, EVAPORATION

> **HOW LONG IT TAKES**
> four to eight hours, including the
> time it takes to make water
> beads absorb water

> **WHAT YOU NEED**
> water beads
> glass baking dish
> water
> food coloring
> glow sticks

Water beads
are made of a
water-absorbing
polymer. They are sold
as a water source for plants. When seed water
beads are placed in water, they can absorb more
than 100 times their weight in water, forming marble-
shaped globes. Over time, they slowly release water back
into their surroundings. Water crystal gel, the absorbent material
in disposable diapers, is the powder form of water beads.

WATER BEADS (CONTINUED)

BONUS

RAINBOW WATER BEADS

• The polymer in the beads will absorb the color in colored water. Pour blue and yellow water into a bowl of water beads, and see what color they come out.

• Color six or seven glasses of water in different colors and add water beads. They will absorb the colors, allowing you to use them to make patterns or layer them into rainbows.

"Ooh!"
—Cole

WHAT TO DO

1 MAKE WATER BEADS: Seed water beads look like tiny hard beads when you get them. But soak them in water for four to eight hours and they absorb the water, becoming jelly balls over time. They are fun to observe, time, and experiment with. Remove the water and watch them shrink, too. They'll shrink faster if laid on layers of absorbent paper towels.

2 SUBMERGE clear water beads in a dish of plain water. Ask a friend to identify what's in the dish. Then ask him to reach into it to prove if he's right. He'll encounter the water beads.

3 POUR THE WATER out of the dish, leaving the beads inside to show what the whole container of beads looks like.

4 SET THE DISH on top of a picture or flat sign. Ask your friend to try to identify the subject of the picture or read the words on the sign. He should have trouble, because the beads are in the way, distorting his view. Now pour water into the container. The beads will seem to disappear, and the sign or picture will become clear.

5 IN A DARK or dim room, submerge some glow sticks in the dish with the water beads. How does this affect their visibility?

WHAT TO EXPECT The water beads are very hard to see when they are covered by water.

WHAT'S GOING ON? The water beds have almost the same refractive index as plain water, so when light comes through them it is not bent, making it almost impossible to see them.

FLOATING WATER MAGIC TRICK

You won't believe this can work.

CONCEPTS

PROPERTIES OF WATER, PHYSICS

> **HOW LONG IT TAKES**
> thirty minutes (including practice time)

> **WHAT YOU NEED**
> a glass of water
> a stiff card
> a penny

My grandfather used to do these tricks in restaurants while we waited for our food. The longer we waited, the more tricks he did. How embarrassing!

It's true that there's no "magic" happening here, just real science. To add magical flair, work on your air of mystery and your interaction with your audience. Consider what to say and do to create the biggest "gee, whiz!" moment.

FLOATING WATER MAGIC TRICK (CONTINUED)

WHAT TO DO

1 PLACE THE PENNY in the glass of water.

2 HOLD THE CARD firmly over the mouth of the glass.

3 FLIP the glass.

> **WHAT TO EXPECT** If you do it right, holding the card very firmly, you'll only lose a little water when you flip the glass. Still, do it on a surface you can stand to get wet, and be prepared to practice a little to get the glass to retain the maximum amount of water.
>
> 1. Quickly slide the card out from under the glass.
> 2. Dry the area around the glass so that it looks like you had no spillage at all.

> **WHAT TO EXPECT THIS TIME** The water will shift down and rest right on the tabletop, held in place by the glass. The penny will appear under the water. But how to get it out? The only way is to slide the card back under again—or just lift the glass and get ready to mop up the mess.

> **WHAT'S GOING ON?** The water in the glass has enough pressure to "hold on" to the tabletop, just as it will hold on to the paper in the Double Bonus on page 15.

BONUS

DISAPPEARING GLASS MAGIC TRICK

This one requires vegetable oil and two glasses, one small enough to fit inside the other. Place the smaller glass inside the larger. Pour vegetable oil into the small glass. You'll be able to see the small glass. Do the next step while looking through the glasses from the side. Continue pouring as the vegetable oil overflows the smaller glass and fills the large one. The smaller glass should disappear from view.

DOUBLE BONUS:
GLASS AND PAPER

Flip a glass of water over a sheet of paper just a little bigger than your glass. As you hold the glass upside down, the paper should stick over the mouth of the glass, and the water should stay inside.

"Why does that work?"
—Sossi

THE WET PENNY

It looks like magic ... but is it?

CONCEPTS

AIR PRESSURE, VACUUM,
COMBUSTION, IGNITION

HOW LONG IT TAKES
twenty minutes, including setup

WHAT YOU NEED
a shallow bowl or dish
a tall water glass
a penny
a cork
matches
a thin knife, skewer, or needle

Here's another demonstration to help you put on a good show. Knowing what happens —the science "magic" behind the show—makes you the true master. Ask your audience what they think is happening before explaining the phenomenon.

OUR TRY

A full day after we finished this experiment, the glass still held the water firmly inside, and the dish and penny were still dry. We even moved it from one table to another without change. In the end, we took it apart to do the dishes, but we wondered how long it would last before some air made its way inside the glass and the water was released back into the dish.

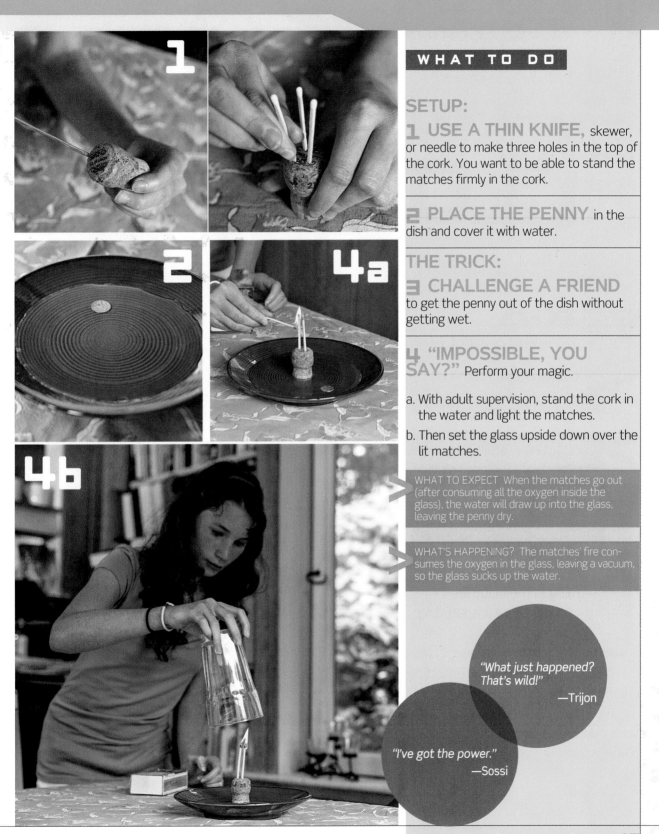

WHAT TO DO

SETUP:

1 USE A THIN KNIFE, skewer, or needle to make three holes in the top of the cork. You want to be able to stand the matches firmly in the cork.

2 PLACE THE PENNY in the dish and cover it with water.

THE TRICK:

3 CHALLENGE A FRIEND to get the penny out of the dish without getting wet.

4 "IMPOSSIBLE, YOU SAY?" Perform your magic.

a. With adult supervision, stand the cork in the water and light the matches.

b. Then set the glass upside down over the lit matches.

WHAT TO EXPECT When the matches go out (after consuming all the oxygen inside the glass), the water will draw up into the glass, leaving the penny dry.

WHAT'S HAPPENING? The matches' fire consumes the oxygen in the glass, leaving a vacuum, so the glass sucks up the water.

"What just happened? That's wild!"
—Trijon

"I've got the power."
—Sossi

SWIMMING WITH CLOTHES ON

It's kind of a drag.

CONCEPTS

DRAG, FLUID DYNAMICS, AERODYNAMICS

HOW LONG IT TAKES
an hour or two

WHAT YOU NEED
a swimming pool
a swimsuit
street clothes
a stopwatch
a notebook
a pair of pants
a partner and adult supervision

Lifesavers practice swimming in their clothes in order to be prepared for how that feels. They need to know how to adapt their swim to deal with the additional drag created by wet fabric. Go beyond "how it feels" by measuring the difference clothes and swimsuits make to the speed of your swim.

NOTE OF CAUTION
Never swim alone.

WHAT TO DO

1 HAVE YOUR PARTNER time your laps.

2 SWIM TEN LAPS, alternating what you're wearing each time. The first lap, swim in your swimsuit.

3 THE SECOND LAP, put on clothes. Decide what clothes you'll wear. You can assess the effects of wearing shoes, jeans, and a sweatshirt, or lighten up a little with shorts and a t-shirt.

4 COMPARE YOUR swimming times with and without clothes.

> **NOTE** You'll get tired—and possibly slow down—as you swim your laps. The purpose of alternating is to try to keep your energy level equal.

> **WHAT TO EXPECT** Your first lap, in the swimsuit, will probably be fastest. Your last lap, in clothes, slowest of all.

> **WHAT'S HAPPENING?** As your clothes fill with water, they will weigh you down. This is increased drag. When you wear your swimsuit, you help make your body more streamlined and aerodynamic, decreasing drag.

"That's 23 seconds with clothes on and 13 seconds with a swimsuit on."
—Doug

QUESTION THIS!

• Which fabrics create the most drag?

• What strokes are easier or harder when you're wearing clothes while swimming?

COLORED CANDY

Candy-coating, revealed

CONCEPTS

SOLUTIONS, SUSPENSIONS, COLORS, PIGMENTS

>> **HOW LONG IT TAKES**
two to three hours

>> **WHAT YOU NEED**
petri dishes
water
clock or timer
colored candies

I like candy. Who doesn't? Who wouldn't like something that is designed for enjoyment, not just tasty, but sweet to the eyes as well. How do they do that? This experiment helps you get to the bottom of the mystery of colorful candy-coating—including the mystery of one favorite candy whose color actually changes as you suck on it.

WHAT TO DO

1 FILL EACH PETRI DISH with water and put a colored candy in.

2 WATCH THE COLORS dissolve at different rates.

3 YOU CAN ALSO experiment with other liquids to see how the colors behave in different solutions, or in liquids at different temperatures.

WHAT TO EXPECT The colors will change at different rates depending on the color, the liquid, and the temperature of the solution.

WHAT'S GOING ON? The solid candy melts into the water or other liquid to create a solution that has its own color. Different pigments (solids used to create colors) dissolve (enter solutions) at different rates.

QUESTION THIS!

• Does it make a difference if the colored candy has a flavor or not?

• Do different candies with the same color dissolve at the same rate?

• What happens to candies that have writing or other symbols stamped onto them?

• What will happen if you place two or more candies of different colors in the same dish? Can you make new colors this way?

"I wonder if Coke or seltzer—something carbonated—would melt the coating of the candy faster?"

—Brandon

BONUS

EXPANDING GUMMIES

Place a gummy bear or other gummy in a petri dish full of water overnight. What happens to it by morning?

OUR TRY

Gobstoppers are particularly great with this because they have layers of colors. We also tried Skittles and M&Ms.

POP ROCKS BLOW UP BALLOONS

Soda not fizzy enough? Try this!

When certain candy combines with soda, the results can be dramatic. For good reason, the experiments here are very popular on TV and the Internet—and there are various theories on what makes them work.

WHAT TO DO

1 POUR THE POP ROCKS into the uninflated balloon.

2 OPEN THE SODA bottle. Set the cap aside.

3 PINCH ABOVE the neck of the balloon to hold the Pop Rocks inside while stretching the neck of the balloon over the bottle neck.

4 RELEASE THE balloon, letting the Pop Rocks fall into the soda. Step back!

WHAT TO EXPECT The balloon should inflate. Janelle's didn't inflate as much as Jarrett's, but it did stand up straight.

WHAT'S GOING ON? Pop Rocks are made from pressurized carbon dioxide, which is a gas. When you place them in your mouth, the moisture reacts with the carbon dioxide, creating little pops. The bubbles in soda come from pumping carbon into the syrup (in a process called carbonation). So the soda also has pressurized carbon dioxide. When you add Pop Rocks to soda, the bubbles that result are big enough to inflate the balloon.

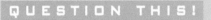

QUESTION THIS!

- What's the smallest number of Pop Rocks that will inflate the balloon?

- Will different kinds of soda have different reactions? How about diet vs. regular?

- How could you increase the amount of inflation you get from this reaction?

CREDITS

Acknowledgments

Our Models: Aaliyah, Abigail, Adriana, Allison, Ariel, Bailey, Brandon, Caitlyn, Cole, Doug, Dylan, Emily, Isaac, Janelle, Jarrett, Jason, Jen, Justin, Lori, Luke, Mae, Marco, Nick, Nikitha, Niyanna, Patsy, Priyanka, Serenity, Sossi, Stephanie, Trijon, Wyatt

Special thanks to Tina Kiniry at the John Casablancas Modeling Agency

All photographs shot on location by Matthew Rakola

Published by the National Geographic Society

John M. Fahey, *Chairman of the Board and Chief Executive Officer*
Declan Moore, *Executive Vice President; President, Publishing and Travel*
Melina Gerosa Bellows, *Executive Vice President; Chief Creative Officer, Books, Kids, and Family*

Prepared by the Book Division

Hector Sierra, *Senior Vice President and General Manager*
Nancy Laties Feresten, *Senior Vice President, Kids Publishing and Media*
Jennifer Emmett, *Vice President, Editorial Director, Kids Books*
Eva Absher-Schantz, *Design Director, Kids Publishing and Media*
Jay Sumner, *Director of Photography, Kids Publishing and Media*
R. Gary Colbert, *Production Director*
Jennifer A. Thornton, *Director of Managing Editorial*

Staff for This Book

Priyanka Lamichhane, *Project Editor*
Angela Modany, *Assistant Editor*
Eva Absher-Schantz, *Art Director*
Lori Epstein, *Senior Photo Editor*
Itzhack Shelomi, *Designer*
Ariane Szu-Tu, *Editorial Assistant*
Paige Towler, *Editorial Intern*
Sanjida Rashid and Rachel Kenny, *Design Production Assistants*
Margaret Leist, *Photo Assistant*
Grace Hill, *Associate Managing Editor*
Joan Gossett, *Production Editor*
Lewis R. Bassford, *Production Manager*
Susan Borke, *Legal and Business Affairs*

Production Services

Phillip L. Schlosser, *Senior Vice President*
Chris Brown, *Vice President, NG Book Manufacturing*
George Bounelis, *Senior Production Manager*
Nicole Elliott, *Director of Production*
Rachel Faulise, *Manager*
Robert L. Barr, *Manager*

The National Geographic Society is one of the world's largest nonprofit scientific and educational organizations. Founded in 1888 to "increase and diffuse geographic knowledge," the Society's mission is to inspire people to care about the planet. It reaches more than 400 million people worldwide each month through its official journal, *National Geographic*, and other magazines; National Geographic Channel; television documentaries; music; radio; films; books; DVDs; maps; exhibitions; live events; school publishing programs; interactive media; and merchandise. National Geographic has funded more than 10,000 scientific research, conservation and exploration projects and supports an education program promoting geographic literacy.

For more information, please visit nationalgeographic .com, call 1-800-NGS LINE (647-5463), or write to the following address:
National Geographic Society
1145 17th Street N.W.
Washington, D.C. 20036-4688 U.S.A.

Visit us online at nationalgeographic.com/books

For librarians and teachers: ngchildrensbooks.org

More for kids from National Geographic:
kids.nationalgeographic.com

For information about special discounts for bulk purchases, please contact National Geographic Books Special Sales: ngspecsales@ngs.org

For rights or permissions inquiries, please contact National Geographic Books Subsidiary Rights: ngbookrights@ngs.org

Dollar Tree edition ISBN: 978-1-4263-2382-9

Printed in the U.S.A.
15/KG/1